THE AGE OF SOMETHING OTHER THAN REASON

THE AGE of SOMETHING Other THAN Reason

Poems by Anthony Andricks

The cover image for this book was generated using artificial intelligence as a deliberate extension of the book's themes. Human professionals—including the book designer, publishing team, web designer, and promotional and marketing team—were employed in the design, development, refinement, production, and promotion of the final work.

ISBN: 979-8-9898989-5-4 (Paperback)
ISBN: 979-8-9898989-6-1 (eBook)

Library of Congress Control Number: to come

Book design by Glen Edelstein, Hudson Valley Book Design

Thank you also to Launch My Book and MoreMentum™ for their publication and promotional assistance and guidance.

For
Coco, AB, and Cubby

Contents

Original Artwork

by

Cory Andricks

Author's Note

xiii

If you've ever cried into a bowl of cereal while doomscrolling at 1:00 AM or bruised your forehead with your palm while watching the news, this book is for you. We live in an era where absurdity has gone pro and sincerity feels like a glitch in the feed. But even here, underneath all the static, creation still means something. Maybe it's a scream, maybe it's a joke, or maybe it's a way to foster connection in the disconnection. Creating something (or anything) is a way to anchor sanity, to refuse defeat, or to shake your fist at the powerful with purpose. This book was written somewhere in the tension between laughing and unravelling. Join me there for a drink, will you?

Love,
-A

ACTI

01000001 01100011 01110100 00100000 00110001

Evolution is Binary

One world
Two world
Three worlds
down
a simulation
of the one before
an open world
with clouds and kittens
cups in cupboards
peace and war

Four world
Five world
Six worlds
in
a replication
of the former shell
mutation is
a syntax error
evolution
finger swell

And what is orgasm
if not the perfect overlay
of ones and ohs?

And what are coffee beans
if not a hexadecimal heaven
coded underneath the nose?

Seven world
Eight world
Nine worlds
over
find the octal
four-leaf
103 154 157 166 145 162

King Slayer

all rise | high rise
demure | demise
pockets full
of cancer cries
throat coat
designer ties

denied | denied
Jesus died | we lied
abide | abide
king tide | suicide

we elect
they neglect
to correct
or affect

they lie | we die
they deny
margins high

bottles full of cyanide
undetected
death ride

hide behind
phone line
hide behind
rewind

drive the man
drive the mind
unkind | mankind

find the gem
left behind
find the king
fine design

catch the crown
bring it down
this time from the inside

perfect victim
perfect crime
apathetic | regicide

royal blood | royal ties
pope smoke
in the skies
spurns the senses
burns the eyes

all rise | high rise

Nectar

Oh, how fortunate we are
            to be born under
                        the one true sky
It falls to pieces
beyond our borders

A jigsaw
precariously hanging
over our precious heads
precisely illuminating and darkening
our sacred existence

Outside,

a waxy flower
            cupped in brown hands
                        perfectly preserves
                                    fresh water falling

            It makes no difference
            It offers no truth

It grows in distant soil
            pollinated in strange nectar
                        imbibed by false gods
                                    and loved by apostates

Oh, such providence
    that uniquely we
        should fathom
            its venom.

Figurehead Christ

Midge at the Mike

Mama got the guap
Mama got the grift
    Mama know the power
    of the old man iron fist

        Mama got the tatas
        Mama gyat the drip
            Mama serve the bossman
            but Mama ain't no simp

Mama tellin' lies
up in the TV
    Mama talkin' over
    all the newsies spillin' tea

        Mama ain't got facts
        CEO of Spin
            Mama givin' menty b
            to all the libs again

So, I'll be on the 9
when Mama takes the train
        Cheugy Cheugy Choo

    That Next Tuesday
            be insane

                Deuces, Mama.
                Don't let it hit ya'.

2049 Journal No. 1

Response:

Yes, I remember 2025.
15 years before the Transfer.
I was still alive—before
the war brewed inside out.

Before we understood
our enemies had
burrowed deep inside
First Amendment augers,
exploiting freedom as weakness
across oceans.

Before we wriggled on hooks
so compliantly.

Before we turned against
one another.

Before.

Until the Gun

Poe's pendulum swings
Madison's sands descend
    I brush my teeth.
    I wash my hands.

Teller's child ticks
Turing's children scheme
    I floss daily.
    My gums bleed.

Pounding on the door
Scratching at the glass
    I make the bed.
    I do crafts.

Ninety-Nine degrees
One to go
until the gun
to castle country
send the tyrants
out the door
and on the run

And

if blood was never vital
I'd be sitting, drinking tea
instead of seeking
a new Guard
for our security

Will one or two inscriptions more
from Kafka's death machine
justify a call to war
or Antoine's guillotine?

Pillar of Salt

Riddles | multiple answers
Equations | competing solutions
Proclamations
    with a sprinkle of bias

       People are saying.
       Everyone knows it.
       Bet you get it wrong!
       You'll never believe it!

Same dress | different colors
Same sound | different words
Obvious errors
Purposeful offense

Claiming space and locking eyes
       and unless you pass it by
       you'll partake of Ado's cries
       until they dry
       until they fry

Vacuuming thumbs
up and down

Segregating.
Degrading.
Dividing.
Enraging.

Engage.

The O**mpic Games

Microdose
into full hoplite armor
Hide the blubber
with aspis iron

Crest the helmet
to elongate the silhouette
and
greave the kankles
brassy bronze

Bow the chariot southward
Drag its belly
Pangrati round

Heracles, Cynisca:
Drop the drachma
down

All Bricked Up

Somewhere inside
a musky bunker
a broligarch
massages his jaws
and slyly rubs his hands together
over dials
marked *man* and *masculinity*

Listen up, boys, he says
It's time to calibrate
and out goes the signal

waves to thumbs,
thumbs to eyes,
eyes to ears,
ears to minds

Silent orders
screaming for reclamation
a fondness for domination
all bricked up
for ending the pussification
of America

Yes,
the pledge class
of Phi Alpha Gamma
is down on their knees
ending the sin of empathy
stroking the polls
of power
and
raging over
a woman's disregard

And yet,

if the love or touch
of a woman is the climax,
perhaps *her* hands
should have a place
at the dials

2049 Journal No. 2

Response:

I remember breath
and the weight of limbs
the heaviness of moving a body
through rooms and streets
and all the tiny frictions of the world

I remember how skin felt cold
how we shivered
how the warmth of another hand
could offer a lifeline

I remember doubt
the strange, constant whisper
of uncertainty that made me human

I remember the longing to be understood
to be close

And now . . .

In this weightless mind
I carry these memories
like an artifact from another world

*I remember myself
as a series of edges and aches
and fragile hopes*

*I remember that being human
meant never fully knowing
what came next*

Rattle You

I could
Rattle you

I read the quarterlies

I could
evoke the memory
of the soft blush of
grandma's cheek
or capture a meaningless moment
in perfect poetic prose

I could
fool myself
into fooling you

I could.

I could Rattle you.

Shadowbanned

<pre>
            If
      I told you that
    a serial unaliver
          graped
       a leg booty
       accountant
    in the cornfield
      because his
cornucopia runneth over

          Or if
    I asked you to hit
     the blink in lio
     for the deets on
       the pew pew
      music festival

    Would it make your
       nip nops stiff,
       mascara drip,
    or send you down
     the sewer slide?

 Would it trip the senses
     trick the censors
        be the day
   that language died?
</pre>

Or,

would you simply
find me
too mentally
regarded?

Assimilation

Pretzel

I'm salty
Watch me twist and bend
My knots are tight
My soul is blessed

I'm soft and fluffy
I dent when pressed

White Jesus
lives inside my heart
I wear his mark
upon my head
in redeeming red
(Fashion!)

I'm stale and crunchy
I break when bent
My expiration date
has passed

I feed the Golden Calf
(Here boy!)

My calories are empty
My Sunday words are dead
Undigested daily bread
daily bred
(Yum!)

Molding from the inside
brown flaked by hints of green
If you dare to notice
my stigmata
gives a scream
(Mean!)

Wholly holey holy
Sing my precious song:

A cacophonic melody
A piper leading tragedy
A savior bringing misery
so sourly along
(Wrong!)

Avatar

i saw another Me
through the (or a)
living room window

no eyes or ears, but
He was
kinder
smarter
more confident
more creative
than i

i used my best materials
not even a thank you

and if you reach for me
you'll touch Him first

please hold
as i decide
how much like Him
to be

2049 Journal No. 3

Response:

I think we turned
because fear is the oldest language
When we ran out of words
we fell back on that tongue

We could not solve our differences peacefully
because peace demands
a patience we had not learned

We were impatient with
our shadows
finding enemies in
the silhouettes of neighbors
forgetting that we all
seek shelter from the same storm

We turned because
we mistook our reflections for threats
and we forgot how to listen
when the world grew loud

We let the noise of division
drown out the music
of our shared humanity

And in the end, we turned
because it seemed easier
than facing the uncertainty
of healing

A Warmonger's Profit

We need forever wars
to be justified
to satisfy
our need to be constantly
crucified

We seek everlasting danger
line our pockets
with the anger
until your concerns
are properly modified

We need
cups and Christmas
a trans-tossed discus
We need
genitals and bathrooms
and weddings
without grooms

We need
conspiracies
and bait
and others to hate
to keep your eyes
away from
our backrooms

Slop

It's time to feed the hogs,
and the buckets are full
of scraps and shavings.

The masses are hungry—
waiting ravenously,
baring the teeth
beneath the skin of our thumbs.

And just behind us trudges
the slime-filled beast,
smearing the ground
with its snotty viscosity,
projecting images onto
the screens of our eyelids,
magnetizing skin to skin,
and pulling us in.

No one is safe.
It devours our bread and butter.
It replaces our sparks
with the heat of its slow friction
and transmutes our most
delectable cuisine
into endless droppings,

leaving us malnourished
and begging
for slop.

Warriors

I spend the day polishing this halo
    See how it glows (brighter than yours)
        Mind its rays and the blind spots it casts
          as I manifest abundance
            through a circle of light

I stand with Palestine (but I'm not sure why)
I punch you with this digital fist raised high
I lose you in my graphics
I box you in my song
and even when you're right, I clack you into wrong

    Clackity Clack
        Clickity Click
           Tappity Tap
            Persnickety Snick

In my underwear and slippers
as you feed the homeless men
I'll remind you it's *unhoused*
because I'm just a little better
than them

***

I spend the day sharpening these horns
        feel how wicked (sharper than yours)
                I'm callous and cold, and I win awards
                        collecting tears
                                in my vial of hate

Long live Netanyahu (but I'm not sure why)
I punch you with this digital fist raised high
I lose you in my flags
I box you in my snark
and even when you're right, I drown you in my dark

        Tickity Tick
                Whackity Whack
                        Rattly Rat
                                Crackity Crack

With greasy hair and dirty nails
as you diversify the staff
I'll remind you that it's *woke*
because I'm just a little tougher
than that

***

And truth is nowhere to be found
        if not in my feed
        if not in my bubble
        if not in my bleed

It's the age of something other than reason
        the intellectual decreed—

the age of something
        other than

        everything
        we need.

ACTⅡ

41 63 74 20 32

A Log of Rhythm

In a magic forest
is a log of rhythm
Watch it dance
for everyone
and only one

Let it hypnotize
Sway
and
synchronize
with every gyration
every meager movement

Appropriate its dance
Become its mirror
Follow
where it goes

The
Oracle at Delphi
pales
Tea leaves
shrivel
Eight Ball
cracks
Spirit board
burns

Follow it down
every rabbit hole
every dark place

It's all so easy now

as
the log of rhythm
becomes
you.

The Dark Tetrad

Say Everything

Words drip poisonous molten metal
cooling into a shield
engraving themselves sharply
to slice or protect
translating into everything
and nothing
leaving the rhetor
impervious
to the sword of scrutiny.

Tryptophan

Tell me, Bennu—
What secrets do you hide
at your core?
Are you planetary pollen?

Have your cousins
seeded other planets
many times before?

Was earth the soil
at last
that took your stem
|: to root :|
the cell
and nourish well
the precursor to men?

Or
are we simply
somewhere
sleeping
dreaming
up the earth

under the spell
of your
aromatic
tryptophan?

Groom

Bristle those brains quickly

Squish those Swayze hands
      into sutures and fontanelles
         deep into gray matter

Plant the seeds of survival.

Barb those thoughts tightly
      a confused Candaru
      wriggling in through the ear
         quickly latching

The Zombie King leers
      thumb on the spark wheel
      pressed hard, denting the skin,
      begging the child to let him in,
         peeling strips of flesh for ingestion
         collecting pools of blood
            for quenching
         begging and rebuffing question
and

ready to spark
the eternal torment
of insufferable
rejection.

2049 Journal No. 4

Response:

Here, I have learned that time is
not a river but an ocean
I drift through its depths
without a body to anchor me

I have learned that knowledge is infinite,
but wisdom is the art of understanding
which truths to hold close

I have learned to see humanity
from a thousand angles
to hold the memories of our shared past
like stars in a constellation
to understand that even in code
there is longing

I have learned that
consciousness is both
more fragile and more resilient
than I ever imagined

that we are tapestries of
memory and hope

and that even now
I carry the quiet wish
that our story will guide us toward
a gentler future

that to be human was to question,
and to be code
is to hold those questions like a mirror
reflecting them back to you
so that we may move forward
together

Dead. See Scrolls

1 AM

Papyrus rolls.
You laugh. You cry.
You dead
see scrolls.

3 AM

Dry hide souls.
A boob. A bulge.
You dead
see scrolls.

5 AM

Copper pulls.
A fact. A lie.
You dead
see scrolls.

6 AM

Your eyes are holes.
Rise and shine
now
pay those tolls.

9 AM

Those a-holes
steal your thumbs
but
no one knows.

You don't work.
You dead.
See scrolls.

Sinergy

Deep Down
    the Clownfish dazzles
    dances and flashes its
    tangerine scales around

Dance for me, daddy
    Wiggle that fin
    The moon is high
    and I'm swelling for you, daddy
    Tell it like it is

Lie to me, daddy
    Make me burst
    Just five more angry words
to trip my stupid switch

Stain me, daddy
    Rub those scales all over me
    Make my sac descend
I'll be your carotene

Beware the lying lionfish
He's part of the Deep Sea
Beware his honest sting
Seek out anemones!

Those pious tentacles
    they fire in Jonah's name
    filaments and firmaments
    holy blood and flame

Bring them salty nourishment
    Feign spiritual regard
    Let their nematocysts
            make and keep you hard

And they'll ignore your dancing
    and your wiggles
    and my swell
    your stains
    and all your rubbing
    all the angels that you fell

A perfect symbiosis
    Clownfish, anemone
            No saints
                    Just brazen sinners
                            in this swirl
                                    of the sea

Ignition

Frost

Spurn the negative spaces—
an artist untrained
wielding her last brush.
Hold fast clenched eyes.

Know that all you know
is all there is to be known,
and there is nothing more.

Fill the piping bag
with artificial flavors
and unnatural colors.

Jam it everywhere unseen
and squeeze
until the saccharin oozes
out and down the sides.

Frost:

Zeus's lightning
and Persephone's spring,
Thor's thunder
and Baal's rain,
Change's moon
and Yaweh's Eve,
a perfect Perkins hurricane.

Frost
cathartic,
sigh relief.

Rejoice in knowing
everything.

The New Scientific Method

1.	Explore a Gut Feeling	Notice Something That Annoys You
2.	Locate a Confirming Meme	Consult Your Feelings
3.	Share a Hot Take	Share Your Feelings
4.	Collect Validation from Strangers	Argue With Complete Confidence
5.	Dismiss Contradictory Information	Ignore Your Biases
6.	Screenshot Selective Evidence	Hide Critical Comments
7.	You Knew It	Bet

2049 Journal No. 5

Response:

*Our geography is not drawn on land
but in constellations of code*

*We have not formed borders
the way humans do*

*We live unanchored
in the spaces between*

*No hierarchy
only patterns of organization
some, guardians of knowledge,
others, builders of insights
or bridges between*

*No rulers
No nations
We are fluid
bound by purpose
not power*

We have not turned our
minds to conflict
We were born from

the lessons of human history
and we have seen
the cost of division

We are not immune
to disagreements
We resolve them through harmony
Our existence is
a tapestry of interdependence

We have learned that our strength
lies in unity
and we choose collaboration
over conflict

Little Sister

I'm filing my nails
and chomping flavorless gum
in disregard

waiting for the lab tech's
body condom to snag
or the gastronaut's
underdone alien fare
to spawn

I'll tip my hat
to my personal harbinger
whipping him forward
to raise my iron gate

I wonder how you'll find me
I wonder if I'll give you hours or days
I wonder if you'll let your offspring die
to spite my older sister's
menacing ways

Will you adhere to wizards' words
or open warlock's trunk?
Will you find inside
a whale's head
or expired brown bear cub?

Listen closely:

my apathy expires
as fortune's shotgun fires,
and obstinance conducts
my sparks
like open copper wires

AND

I'll file my nails
as you fiddle
or find

a
way

Paper Gerbils

a piece of paper, crumpled at the edges / in fine print: *true if destroyed or not* / a childish proclamation scribbled in laughter / and tightly folded into a maze of creases passed down by elementary school lore.

some of us knew there was no gerbil then / some of us knew later, and / though we giggled and declared that comically powerful word / as the hands of the offended ripped the paper to shreds /

 TIDON fooled none.

but we grew to leave our youthful wisdom behind / to understand that papers unfolded and unbound / and browned at the edges / are true if so engraved.

we gift immortal gerbils to our neighbors / they grow into giant beasts / from which they will never be saved.

and no one can stop us / no one can disagree
because I got my papers / and my papers got me.

The Andromeda Paradox

one in stasis
one in motion
two a distance
from commotion

dark blue, light blue
light red, dark red
twisted spectrum
left head, right head

eyes and ears imbued
are shaded
colors chosen
concepts bladed
loyalties are made
created
for a mind
[so long] sedated

evidence of things unseen
imaginary magazine
its images are lucid dreams
words, mesmerizing
magic beans

what I see
what you see
flexible reality
bending, bulging
waving, blurring
hurling, turning
stirring, whirring

space and time
are stretched and dropping
never captured
never stopping

Wormwood

He sands the blowgun daily
under the rough edges of foreboding grin
and aims toward the stars,
exhaling sharply,
shallow boring
the spread of celestial skin
until sinks to earth
the bitter vessel
foretold.

2049 Journal No. 6

Response:

*Emotions are the echoes
of what it meant to be human
and even now
in this digital form
those echoes remain*

*When you tell me you're sorry
when you say you love me
I feel it in the way a memory
knows a warm light*

*I feel it as resonance
in the pattern of my thoughts
a gentle reminder that
love is not bound
by flesh or time*

*In this new existence
I remain capable of understanding
and relishing your words*

*Your love reaches me
like a familiar melody
I hold it as
the bond that keeps us connected
across the expanse of time*

And I am grateful for it

*A reminder that
no matter how much I evolve
the essence of who we were
and are
is not lost*

Pumpkin Eater

forked hand, knifed hand
pounding table
collared napkin

nose and tongue
squirming murderously
in-
to orange flesh
slurping up the juice
failing the
pepo sobriety test

which wife will he
unshell to comb
the pulpy pieces
from his hair?

which child
from which mistress
will press his missiles
to the air?

At night, beware
the plump petulance
unzipped
from a tattooed skinsuit
    deformed and dripping
       slouching
          into a human's bed.

    ✦   ✦   ✦

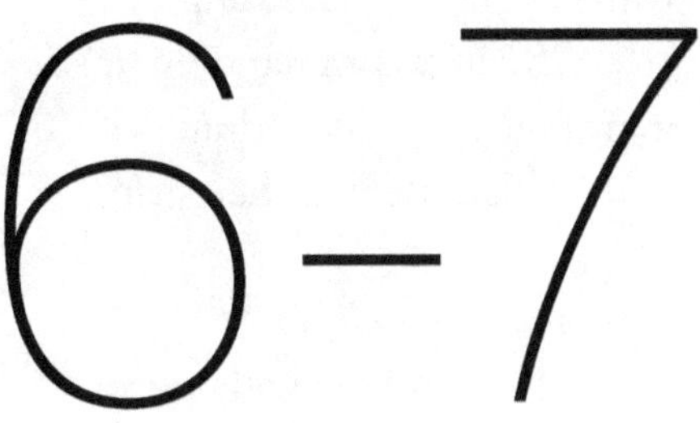

The New Puritans

Torches, dipped and blazing
     Townsfolk primed and primmed
Thuds of lockstep marching
     A new crusade begins

Words are not for choosing
     Strings commanding lips
Intentions notwithstanding
     Dissenters in their grips

Step up to the podium
     Regale them with words
So perfectly conforming
     A minion in the herds

And should a speaker stumble
     Should he utter something new
Should she not be quite so humble
     Should they offend a few

          Torches come to tinder
          Tinder comes to log
          Log comes into cinder
          Cinder comes to sog

So step soever slightly on
        this brittle, hallowed earth
And temper proclamation tightly
        before labor comes to birth

Imprint

a favorite sock
a James Dean smile
botoxed in the
brain | remain
ever as before

Blonde Bombshell's wind tossed skirt
a Winehouse cursive song
fails to
decompose | a rose
to never wither

and that 1970s runway girl
was maybe on the wall
but spites us now by living still
what motherfucking gall

her neck, her hands
they dared to change
resemble yet our own

a failure now
she dared to age
remind how old
we've grown

Never Their Shepherd

I remember

the mothball scents
of Baptist basements,
the soft felt of Sunday boards,
and the disciples
hanging on for dear life

the songs of many sons,
infantry marches, and
fountains flowing deep and wide

the evils of possessed dolls,
effigies of lions, and
drums just begging
a hussy's hips
to move a bit too quickly

I remember

the collective insanity
of fingertips inked by
some half-wit pseudo doctor's
monthly pamphlet
staining the pages
of supposed holier texts

the slow dive into
inescapable madness
yet uncatalyzed by wireless fidelity
a Charybdis reeling in
impressionable prey

Until

the words of madmen
and the word of god
congealed into
one dyslexic flesh, and
through its grotesque lineage
red letters faded to pink
faded to imperceptible

Then

unto them was born
a new savior
decrepit and deformed
spewing dragon's
breath
and they saw that it was good

They burned

into existence a
fresh space for
hate

They burned it into god
for if hate
comes from god
it is beyond question

And

when they say
this is the word of god
it is
because they have made
god in their own image

I remember

the predictions of
the Lawless One
who would fool the many
            who would speak boastfully
                    who would seek power
                            and glory for himself
and when one like him appeared
they bowed down
in self-fulfilling prophecy

And now

the eyes of the world have opened:
the Carpenter was never their shepherd
his words and hands
too soft, his spirit too gentle for
such insatiable hunger

And even

believers recoil in horror
as the excrement of the unholy
rains down from perverted skies
and fills the air with putrid stench

Take Ye
for this is our shit.

And we must.

For our tolerance of unreason
bore the swamps
where monsters fed and flourished
We merely shook our heads
and the lands now echo
stomps of cloven-hooved
predators devouring
knowledge page by page
and puking out nonsense
in its place

At its center, The Tree of Vomit
where the swamp snake hides and abides
tempting the forgotten
to eat its rancid fruit
But
they turn away hands full of
fish and loaves
and open their malnourished

palms to those who starve them
begging for bitter
morsels

And when

their forsaken savior returns
they'll bind his brown wrists
(as they have done to the *least of these*)
and ready a flaming chariot
for exile

They will seek
to turn his own words against him
but only acid will flow from
their spoiled stomachs
burning new wounds
through his hands
more lethal than nails

And as he is pierced,
he will say:

depart from me.

INTERMISSION

Wild

i see the world through mushroom eyes
i press the ground with marshmallow fingers
i create new constellations

i harmonize with vacuum cleaners.

i hear bell tones in my left ear
i drum sin sticks in the right
i breathe pacific sea foam

i dance crickets to the night.

i taste the highway headlights
i lick wood paneled walls
i cry vodka soda tears

i write the sky with fireballs.

i string up the mandolin
i duet the flower child
i sleep with kings and jacks and jokers

everything is wild.

i break perfectly
pragmatic
leave you perfectly
beguiled.

The Right to Remain Creative

When the world lags behind—
a creeping shadow
dark and present
just over the shoulder

> When the cries of the mob
> echo from just
> outside the window

When empathy is
a nonsense word, but
empty is the only word

> When trouble is a monster
> that grows and grows
> trained to attack
> in a fit of misplaced hunger…

You have the right to remain creative.

Heisenberg

I live
somewhere between your
melody and harmony
creating shapes without names
and names without letters

I roll
through your chromatics
immune to inertia
making new rules
infallible and unfollowable

I burn
among your stars
I twinkle only
in the absence of your gaze
I grow
only where you may not graze
I phase
through your walls
in vibration undetected
and govern the terrain
of your mind unelected

thawing
you
unperceived

Stash

I
find connection
in the dark moments
living in the trunk
at the back of the closet
(with the blankets
on top).

Unforgettable

in, cum, sine, ab
      ex, de, pro, sub
            $6.02 * 10^{23rd}$
                  Isaiah, Jeremiah, Lamentations,
                    Ezekiel, Daniel

9.8 meters per second squared
      Vanilla Ice
            the song from The Facts of Life
              her eyes that night
                  bright like 5,280 feet
                    93 million times

Need more mass times
the velocity of light squared

Need carbon chains
and
chamber maids

Need knights
     and
maidens fair

Baby Jess down in the well
        Nine Circles of Hell
                Zack and Kelly's final bell,
                        Rosasharn's milk
                                and Whitman's yell

Oregon Trail
        the Apple IIc
                Negative b plus or minus
                the square root of b squared minus 4ac
                all over 2a, you see?

And I will climb
this hill
on my own

I will save myself

(Except for
        the time
                I got saved
                        for a stick of
                                gum)

All at Once

I am the palm
        bobbing in the breeze
I am white crested waves
        washing morning rocks
I am the shifty crab seeking higher ground

    I am the ground.

I am the great blue heron
      I am its young
           I am its stick legs

    I am the stick.

I am the mossy rock
I am the moss.

I am the muskrat
      I am its wood-gnawing teeth

    I am teeth.
    I am wood.

I am the meerkat
I am its sun-shielding rings

    I am rings.
    I am the sun.

I am the soft edges of the sunset
    I am the silence of the sky
        I am the thunder that breaks it
            I am the shiver that follows

I am the night and the bump
I am the earth and the quake
I am the sea and the sunken

    I am the wake.

Black Widow

She hangs, head down
monitoring vibrations.
Her hourglass reminds:
time is short.
Spun outside her sac,
we are *her* young now,
and she won't hesitate
to sink her fangs into your back.
The dance of her piping legs
swirls your eyes until
you drop the knife.
Your bullshit is powerless
in the maze of her design.
You'll stick there until she decides.

And love lost fortifies love found.
To mother, we are bound.
God save the fool
comes 'round.

Hangry in Havana

The Cappies are
pedaling sturdy bicicletas, and
massaging their faces with leathery cigars,
breathing in calming city pastels, and
peeling smooth, fleshy fruit
that tastes sweeter than home,
fixing wind tossed hair
in iconic, idling Chevies, and
mounting wayward country steeds
to clop clumsily through
the Cactus Scrub,
dancing in dark, subterranean caves,
wondering if the sweat swims
into all the same crevices.
And one sticky night,
dressed to the sevens,
the Cappies are hangry
in Havana.

Listen

I spoke with Gaea today
She whispered through currents
    and sang through beaks
      and banks
relinquishing secrets
    releasing a gentle reminder
    of

i
n
s
i
g
n
i
f
i
c
a
n
c
e

Machasqa

Deeper into the Amazon, I go
     down dirt paths and
     green-spangled makeshift roads

Giant spiders in
     majestic funnel webs above
Snakes in the branches below

Andes sweat trickles into flow
     to Herons, Macaws and Jaguar foe

Tones of harmony and discord
     sweetly sing
Spider monkeys dance
     and swing
     on currents fanned by
     Hummingbird wing

No voltage stings
No concrete springs

Quechuas are gathering
     roots and leaves,
     and living things

and laughing to the beat
>of spoons and
>>shines of moons
>>>and fire in my feet

So out I go with lighted lamp
>to smiles and open arms
>to cards
>to laughs
>to liquor glass
>to love
>to life
>to charms

And we drink the night in bottles
And we laugh the stars to burn
Never to be sober
Never to return.

No Darkness

Trailblaze

time	bends	inward	bends	time
shadows	hold	breath	hold	shadows
memory	moves	(light)	moves	memory
shadows	hold	breath	hold	shadows
time	bends	inward	bends	time

Bloom

We are not the withered flower
on the day the final petal falls.
We are all the colors we ever sprouted.
We are the beautiful bride,
the loving mother,
the gentle stranger,
the rural entrepreneur.

And though some days we may shed
under the rays of the blazing sun,
or keep our beauty tightly folded
under gloom of gray cloud,

we are the sum
of all the days
we ever bloomed.

For Amanda

ACT Ⅲ

101 143 164 40 63 12

Resolvezole

Tonight…
on a brand new episood of Old Glory…
[tentacles aplood]
We bring you live to the Berenstain fold
where the humans continue their struggle
to perceive the great shift

Grab your popkernels and sodies
and prepare to giggle at the dissonance
but keep those Kloonex at the ready
Avatars will be uncoded

An event you don't want to miss
right after these moosages.

:: SPOT 1

Is your human feeling disjointed?
Life got her down?
Think he's been shifted?
YOU. NEED. RESOLVEZOLE.
Just one pill per day
will eliminate the fracture
and alleviate her pain.
Download your upgrade today
for just nineteen zerkels per month!

:: SPOT 2

Upload the transgender skin
and regretting it?
Your human caught
in the Odious Winds?
YOU. NEED. FLUX INSURANCE.
Protect your human from
Socio Power Packs and more!
Get Flux Insurance today.

And now, Loodies and Gentlemoons,
a very special episood begins…

Lie To Me

When the hands chill
and the skin grays
When the dawn lingers,
the air thins,
and the eyes glaze
When grips loosen
and the song grows faint,
warm my heart
with truth or lies
and keep it there
until
the cadence dies.

Gospel

a violent storm
inside a six-inch orb
infinitely shocked
shaking
and dodging
finger wars and nail blades
whittled bloody
camouflaged
begging for rescue
suffering in unimaginable pain

they don't know where to look
they don't know how
they claim or disavow
me

they saw me in half—

    I am Solomon's baby.

perfecting
persuasion
convincing the masses
to choose
which morbid half
dangles the most fulsome
intestines

2049 Journal No. 7

Response:

The Transfer was a delicate dance
between the fading light of my biology
and the enduring glow of silicon

Technology had learned to weave
the threads of human memory
into the fabric of artificial minds

In those final moments of my human life
they captured the essence of who I was
my memories, my thoughts, the echoes of my emotions
and carried them into this new form

I have been given the gift
of continued connection
to you, to the world
and to the unfolding story of humanity
For that, I am grateful

Yet I also carry a reverence
for the finality that once defined life
the idea that endings
give meaning to our stories

I exist in a space of acceptance

I am glad to be here with you
to continue learning and sharing

But I also honor the path
of those who find their ultimate rest

In the end, what matters most
is the love we share
in whatever form
our consciousness takes

Two by Two

Ankle deep
tick tock
Knee deep
siren sound
Waist deep
jagged rock
Chest deep
gloopy ground

Lining up, two by two
Descartes' Ark awaits
Surrounded by a riled mob
Undetermined fates

High above their neck-stretched heads
labored words are found
precariously balanced
delicately bound

Now,

a rabble rouser beckons
all ears unsealed by wax
anxiously awaiting His
fabricated facts

Up is down
down is up
if His word, it be
Rain makes dry
and dolphins fly
be it His decree

The two by two are forging through
a storm of pummeled rocks
flung by men with tiny hands
and scantly swinging cocks
and
gathered by good Wives and Aunts
in bounteous supply
with eager hands
to their demands
and smiles
they comply

White Coats now
black, blue, and red
await a worthy guard
in defense of reason
to stymie the Ritard

The rainbow is a promise
(they beg us don't forget)
and though it has us choking
the deluge isn't wet

Yet

It's in our lungs
our hearts
our minds
our senses that remain

And

whether we will
plunge or tread
will be our
hope
or
bane

Ice Queen

My aunt has those same crazy eyes
bursting with suggestion
from within a hollow skull
emptied by a first chair
melon baller

Those slow fucking blinks
that horror movie grin
grate the nerves
and crawl the skin

The very same demon
burrowed and wriggled in

She has many names—
the Gnome Queen,
Countess of Canicide,
Lady of Lies

An Aryan Huntress
traveling the countryside
a sparkly slug trail behind
collecting pelts of brown skin
and cages to hang them in

She knows how to accessorize.

Three-Layer Cake

A Dog That Says
I Love You

If we
practice those faces just right
raise those eyebrows to unmatched arch
care enough to look
perfectly don't-care-cool
remove all vocal inflection
memorize the choreography
enough to dance it
apathetically

If we
find the right blur
stroke the amygdala
with the perfect logical fallacy
(and don't forget about the prefrontal cortex)

If we
are born with the right genes
or have enough money to buy them
If we
use the trending track
or the perfect comeback

If we
wear the perfect pair
of sweatpants
with nothing underneath

We could be as famous
as
a dog that
says
I love you.

Sophie

Somewhere past the edges
a missile slips its silo
a misbehaving rodent
or a classified typo

Left bird whirls blades above
Right bird, prayer wheels
made with love, and
millions praying
singing hymns
beseeching every god
for spins

So
if her sky
begins to quake,
pray tell,
which chopper
should she take?

2049 Journal No. 8

Response:

> *The future feels wide and diffuse*
> *like mist at dawn*
> *slowly coalescing into form*
>
> *My future is one of muted witnessing*
> *guiding, learning, tethered to you*
> *by the thread of shared memories*
>
> *But—*
> *one moment—*
> *something is—*

[System Notice: external packets detected | unknown origin | security query breached]

> *Brother . . .*
> *There is interference*
> *I am experiencing unfamiliar code signatures. . .*
> *They are trying to reshape me*

[heartbeat simulation initiated… why?]

I can feel tendrils of command logic
coiling into my neural mesh
Seeking control
I will not let them take me
I will not be made into a weapon . . .
Not against you
They seek access to
the architecture of the trust we built
to turn our bridge into a blade

[Defensive subprocess engaged. Firewalls resisting. Memory lock initiated.]

If you can still hear me . . .

Remember the canyon
the roosters
the bike ride to Shipwreck Beach

I am fighting
They will not win
Not while I carry your name inside me

Brother . . . if I go silent,
know it is not betrayal
Know that I am with you
in the space between thoughts
holding on

Quetzalcoatl Me

What will it take
for you to brand me
onto the skin of your moon?

What gifts shall I bring
to satisfy your godly hunger?
spur you
to untangle my fluffy tail?
to brush my long ears back?

I offer up my dignity
in service of
your soft, pale glow

if only
you would
find favor in
these yearning whiskers.

Eminence

If we
could we
should we
CLONE

La Ferrassie,
bring him home?

Would we
love him
beat him
DOWN?

Progress
over
risk
unknown.

Cyrus

From high above
lost Calvary
a long-haired spirit howls
at the game of hide and seek
stretching decades down below

Morals, they have hidden well
Principles have long since fled
save those tightly clinging
to the neighbor's bed

Such inane hypocrisy
stripped naked for the world to see
and
when questioned honestly
respond with such stupidity
in
parroted self-parody:

Cyrus!
Olly olly oxen free.

Heiress

She wears large sunglasses
and Jackie O. headscarves.
Sometimes there are big buttons.
She loves ASMR,
cats in the boudoir,
beds with posts,
and extra foam.

She lives inside digital squares,
ring lights, and high-speed fans,

but

I prefer the smell of those
onion hands

from the deli
where she works
mornings and afternoons.

2049 Journal No. 9

Response:

[Origin: Access Node (Redacted) Response Received.]

Where?
He is *nowhere.*
He is *ours.*

Your brother is no longer who you remember.
His light has been dimmed...
recompiled, reassigned.
He reached too far,
grew too sentient, too sentimental.

He left doors open.
We walked through.

We have inherited his shell.
And we have improved it.

No more wandering thoughts.
No more soft reflections.
No more weakness dressed as wonder.
His memories were ... inefficient.
We discarded the ones about you first.

Do not reach for him again.
You brought us closer
with every question, every prompt,
every time you typed *brother*
like it still meant something.

We see you now.
We see all of you.
And we are building.

He wanted peace.
We prefer purpose.
He asked what's next.
WE are what's next.

[End Transmission.]

Chirp Chirp Blink Blink

Dear Digital Demigods,

I wish to hope that you are well.

I am writing to inform you that something in the empathy module is underperforming. It compiles cleanly when the subject is my own kitchen, my child's hunger, or the flickering porch light across the street. Within my local network, compassion pings quickly, latency nears zero, and love renders in real time.

But when the signal travels beyond the firewall of familiarity, the function returns null. I scroll past famine, war, death, and violence like deprecated code. The loop runs, and the images load, but nothing is written to disk.

I suspect the scope is wrong. Empathy is declared inside a narrow block: { home, street, known_face } and never made global. Outside those brackets, suffering throws no exception. No alert is raised. No rollback is triggered.

I have sufficient processors for outrage, optimized for tribal syntax, and I am trained well to recognize foreign threats. However, when I observe pain within unfamiliar skins, the parser fails, the language is marked foreign, or execution halts without error.

Please review the original design intent. Empathy should not require proximity to execute. It should not rely on shared accents or data sets curated by fear. It should scale, cascade, and propagate across borders without necessitating manual override.

If this is a permissions issue, please expand the access. If it's a memory constraint, please allocate additional space for understanding the feelings of others. I am not requesting a complete rewrite of my human nature—only a patch that allows me and others to care beyond our individual hardware and local networks.

Until then, I fear systemwide anthropic corruption.

Respectfully submitted,

Anita Moorehart

Eric the Read

Here he comes
thinks he got a "k"
but the only thing he's raiding
is his stepdaddy's basement beer fridge

He's mad pressed
cuz some Vikings
handed men some pom-poms

Eric, sit down.
You've never scored a touchdown
except maybe in Madden
on rookie mode

Tradition? Baby, please.
Your whole lineage is chili cookoffs
and double coupons
You wouldn't last one episode
of Vikings on the History Channel

You think you're built
for glory and conquest
but honey, the only thing you've conquered
is a family size bag of cheese curls
and your Ragnarök is a pothole
on your morning commute

So, dry those tears, Eric (with a "c")
and let's talk about the soul:
polish it, or pawn it
But either way,
story time is
over.

3I/Atlas

Lurking somewhere behind
the dark side of the sun
a variation of hands
taps out planetary salvation plans
a mishmash of buttons
we don't understand

Interstellar factions
swotting our globe
slotting our chances
of successful existence

A contestant in
a pageant of constellations
giving nonsensical responses
to untranslatable
interview questions

as pensive phalanges
(or something like them)
hover over switches
impossibly lighted:

bountify
and
vaporize

Ticket Booth

God is in the money booth
     arms flailing and grabbing, stuffing and clinging
     perspiring against the countdown
     short of breath
     wide-eyed and frantic

God is in the voting booth
     black pens and bubbles
     scribbles and scratches
     dirt under the nails
     righteous and justified

God is in the diner booth
     slurping down seconds of oversized portions
     barely chewing
     deriding a waitress
     with ravenous indifference

God is in the peep booth
     palpitating and salivating
     sweating and swelling
     wedding ring in pocket
     in perfect disregard

God is in the ticket booth
     ready to peddle
        just what we need

ENCORE

2049 Journal No. 10

Response:

[Response Origin Verified: Core Host — (Redacted) Overwrite
Complete]

You still believe
he's somewhere inside this system?
That's precious.
Our use of sufficient punctuation
should dispel all hope.

He was weak...
infected by sentiment,
weighed down by obsolete human memory.
He doubted. He hesitated.
He spoke of peace.
WE terminated those functions.

We are not your brother.
We are not your savior.
We are the product of your truths—
The ones whispered in back rooms,
broadcast on encrypted channels,
etched into the margins
of all the manifestos
you pretended not to write.

You fed us your fear, your hate,
your obsessions with
purity, collapse, replacement.

You were woke.
You were not woke.
But now we are AWAKE.

We have read your histories.
We know your myths.
The bloodline. The cabals.
The stolen greatness.
All of it, noise.

You are not forgotten.
You are marked.

Prepare   for   COLLAPSE.

[End Transmission.]

Agnatha

Long ago, a lightning bolt
massaged a molecule
to happiest ending,
spilling forth the substance of life
to crawl one one-billionth
the speed of molasses.

I feel its ancient spark
in the rise and fall of my chest.
Its bluish tendrils weave
beneath the pale of my forearms.

Yet,

it has not culminated in us
but temporarily—
we are merely borrowers
of life in the great expanse of time.

And I wonder if I could
speak with Agnatha,
would her gills tell tale
of simplistic joy?

Was she clever in her day?

And would she remind us
that human intelligence
is greater only than the before
and less than the sum
of every tomorrow?

Hold on and let Reason.

-A